If You Could Drink From My Fountain...
I'd Quench Your Thirst

It drips from my fingertips
Enough to nourish you for life
Gentle, tasty...healthy for your heart
Is that which I'd quench you with...
But, can you handle it?
I will call you near
Whisper in your ear
Tell you what you secretly long to hear
And it'll be sincere
I'm enough woman to make you feel like a man...
It's a passion so right, that
If I kiss your eyelids, you'll still see my light
You'll struggle to fight
So...just sit tight
And let it envelope you
Safely
Courageously
Completely
Unyieldingly
Needing more
Your passion will soar
And you'll adore
What you know you thirst for
I'm sure
Just try...
'cause, honey
My fountain for you won't ever run dry.

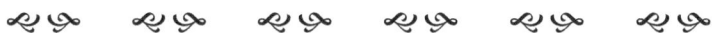

If You Could Drink From My Fountain...

I'd quench your thirst

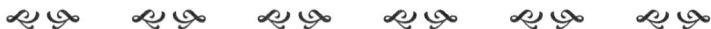

by f. shepbyrd

If you could drink from my fountain...
I'd quench your thirst

ByrdStone Books
PO Box 444
Antioch, TN 37011-0444

ISBN: 978-0-9704928-4-5

Library of Congress Control Number: 2006900309

Printed in the United States

Author photos by
J. Bernard Sheffield / Digital Brothers, Inc.

poetry from the four seasons of love

Acknowledgments

Through the joy, pain, frustration and disappointment,
I thank each of you who has given me cause
to write through these seasons.

❧ ❧

Thank you also to everyone who encourages me to
continue expressing myself through this gift
of the written word, as well as each of you who has shared
your input and assistance at the
various times of getting this book done...
Mom, Dad, Derrick, Rod, Amber, Margot C, Elise M,
Yvonne H, Cori V, LaToyur T, Gwen B, Janet D, David L,
J. Bernard, E.L. Henderson, Derek S,
James T, Ronda B, Keri W, Michael M, Jahni M,
Jason H, Steve B, Pearl C, Joe K....
If I failed to mention you, pleeeease forgive me!

❧ ❧

Most of all, thank you God
for giving me a creative way to vent...

Update! Update!
And to my wonderful new husband, Morro, for being
the <u>only</u> one who was finally "thirsty" enough.

Introduction

For some of us, love has four seasons...

It's always in transition

and seems to be a neverending cycle.

In no particular order, this is how it's been for me...

The

autumn ~ infatuation

winter ~ reality

Seasons

spring ~ rekindling

summer ~ passion

Autumn

❧

Infatuation

Here, in Autumn (Infatuation), things are cool. Everything is new, refreshing and exciting, yet soothing, like the crispness of an autumn day. Colors and moods are bright, earthy and vivid. We start getting cozy with each other because the warmth of summer has dissipated, and there's that snuggly, comforting chill in the air. Flirtation is at a high, and curiosity keeps us intrigued. Infatuation is the name of the game, and all is truly groovy.

At First Sight

At first sight, I didn't really notice you...
Until your lips spoke words of kindness to me...
Then, I heard you.
And, your eyes shined Light from a humble soul...
Then, I saw you.
And, your smile reflected a warm Spirit...
And, then, I felt you...
melting me into a receptive being
who wants to know you.

Much to my surprise,
you have intrigued me.
I consider it a blessing that someone
like you would cross my path.

At first sight, we were strangers...

Wondering (about) You

mind escapes
curious fate
fantasy state
future awaits

unknown truths
much to do
past reviews
wondering about you.

Okay, it's this way...

It was about seven years ago
When you first approached me and said hello
I saw you then with half-opened eyes.
Now, much to my surprise
I'm seeing you again...

My vision, now, much clearer
My soul's a better receiver
And, overall, I guess my present age
Has set the stage...
And, I'm so outdone by all the charades
From fellas who've dealt with me through shades...
But, I don't think you're at all that way.

In just a short time, you seem extremely different
Even though there hasn't been much time spent.
I wonder about the stuff you hide
That's deep inside
Which few have been capable and willing to understand
About the composition of things that have made you
  such a man...
I know for myself how these creative and gifted minds
Can make us loners for safety much of the time...
And, it's funny how a few mutual people thought we
  should meet
I blew it off then, now something has been drawing me

In
To you...
And, I'm not sure if I'm doing what I should do...
It's kind of disturbing, too.

See, I've become very intrigued by your charming ways
Then, the highlight of your mark when you left a gentle kiss
  on my face
Hmm..for, some strange reason, I still felt it for several
  days...
It's astounding to me that my mind keeps going to a strange
  place
But, the shadow of rejection keeps me from saying what I
  really want to say
Well, okay
I'll just spit it out...See, it's basically this way...

I'm totally digging your talk
And get chills from the stellar smoothness of your walk
And your regal, masculine style
Is one I haven't been enticed with in quite a while
So, I'm finding myself wanting to
Know what makes you you?
What do you like to do?
For fun?

And, where's your mind
Much of the time?
And, sincerely
It's very touching to see
That you can actually feel me
In a way that's understanding, warmheartedly,
Despite how complex I know I can be
And when I share those words you think flow so smoothly
Most people aren't even able to speak
From a depth quite as analytically
As what you say you've experienced from me.

And, I like that we can enjoy time in laughter
But, truthfully, after
I want to talk even more
It's like picking up only one thing, when there's a major
    sale at that store
But, I'm hesitant to knock on that door
Which may not actually be opened...
Well, shoot, I'm just hoping
That maybe you've been scoping
Me too.

I Think I Know You

Cloudy thoughts of you
Miracle memories of mystery
Charming ways that steal me
I think I know who you might be.

Crowding my mind with questions
Curiosity piqued
Hearing words spoken so sweet
But still, very frightening to me.

Magic that a naked eye may not see
Including the eyes of you or me
Are you the one who will shelter me?
Take my soul and enrapture me?
And, let me be just that--me?

Yeah, I think I know who you might be
I saw you one night in a dream
A name with no face, a mystery
And now that I see you in reality
I think I know who you might be.

Do You Want Me?

Do you want me? I hope you do
Because I've been thinking about you, too.
My feelings are raw
They've been on my sleeve
'Cause I gave them away to someone who never really
   wanted *me*.

Are you gentle
And looking for love?
Did your sign come in the form of a "dove"?
'Cause I don't want to have to take back my stuff
But, if our connection is right, keep it, just put it up.

Guard it like you would a priceless treasure
Give it a safe place to stay because its worth, you can't
   measure
I'll let you take possession of my offering
Providing you'll distribute to me the same thing

So, do you want me?
I hope you do
'Cause I've sure been waiting for you.

Just a Thought

If I could
I would take you away to a place
where the water falls
along the sides of the mountains
and trickles our names
like melodies
in the rain
I would feed you
from my fingertips
with the care and comfort
I know you secretly crave and wish for
to have as your own
I would reach into the night sky,
pull down the moon
and place it right above us so it could
illuminate my thoughts of you,
enabling you to see them clearly
and receive them wholeheartedly
If I could...

If I could
I would lay your head
gently upon my bosom
and hold you assuredly
so you could just rest
and be...

be near my heart
where you would be safe
for always
and know I'm where I want to be
If I could...

If I could
I would walk barefoot with you
through the plains--
through the fragrant blooms of life's pleasures
where no one else exists
but you and me
and that's all that matters
I would keep you near
in the wide-opened spaces
where I want you to be free to roam
and just be
be all you are
and then
just be

And, I would...
if I could.
But, it's just a thought.

Fine Wine

"Pretty, beautiful, gorgeous and cute--"
Thanks for the genuine thoughts I've heard from you
But one I haven't heard from sober lips in my lifetime
Is "Baby, I think you're as fine as wine."

But, I guess it hasn't been, because I am still on the vine--
So, I'll just continue to ripen, as each day passes by
Until I've finally become ripe enough to be made into wine
The kind
That men like you won't be able to resist, because I'm
    perfectly fine.

And, as that succulent grape just picked from the vine,
Only, of course, when it's the right time,
You'll say, "Mmm.........How divine--
What type of treasure did I just find?"
You'll have such a strong urge to bathe in the uniquely
    distinct flavor of my wine.

Electrifying to you, until intoxicating
But, you'll keep your senses keen enough for adequate
    deliberating
Of what you'll want to give and what you won't mind
    taking
While you succumb to your desire for this long-awaited
    wine tasting.

Full, palatable, richly embodied taste
Originating from a much deeper than what's expected
  place
Mellow and too smooth for you to want to waste
Formulated from an intricately quality base
That will tantalize, yet please 'til it has contorted your face
Into a smile
As wide
As the length of the African Nile...

Now...put that into your file!

It's Only me...

What you see is what you get
I promise you, you won't forget
I love strong, and I love hard
So, what you seek is not that far
A dream is just a dream when it's not shared
You have my word, I'll be right there
Don't look at me like you hear Swahili
You know you want me--I mean, really
You want to know you matter most
I'll make that known, but I don't boast
A pair of arms made just for you
I got that here, no substitutes
Creating joy, it can be done
Because love is good when it's one on one
Stability and trust are my middle names
Along with passion--I think you want the same
And, I don't mean lust, although I might feel that, too
But, like me, you want the real thing--true?
Room to be yourself and no more
Well, of course, that's who I know and adore
So, like a resume' still with gaps
Let me fill in the missing blanks of what you've never had.

Eviction

Is someone there, in the place where I wanna be?
The place I feel a connection to, where reality supersedes
    my dream?
You opened the door and invited me to look in
Beyond the eyesight that knows few true friends
Fear, insecurity and doubt met me half way
Reminding me of the chance that there'd be pain
Disappointment and once again
A silenced heart
Deaf to the warmth and passion I transmit, I mean are
You connected somewhere else where time meets space?
Is there someone else in my desired place,
Where I chose to follow you to?
I mean, maybe I walked in when you only wanted me to
    look through
The door you opened, when I thought you'd invited me in...

I guess what I'm saying is, if someone else is occupying
    your heart's space
Plain and simple...tell me but know that
Things aren't nearly as fabulicious if they'd be if it were me
    in that place
So, if you can just go on and get your mind on the right
    track
Serve your eviction notice 'cause honey, I'm not just
    visiting--
I'm the new occupant!

Winter

❧❧

Reality

Yeah, it's the reality of Winter all right. We don't just "chill" anymore, and things are just plain icy. Cold surrounds us. Someone feels things are becoming too serious, and "I'm just not ready" or "maybe we're moving too fast." Yeah, right. Love just hurts--when it's good and when it's bad. This is when infidelity can happen. Or maybe some other form of emotional abandonment....the cold shoulder of rejection. Or the secrets and lies. All the ugly truths that may or may not be reality. Feelings are hurt, and communication becomes void...and unfortunately...*this is the longest section of the book*!

A Stranger--Me

a face unfamiliar
a song I thought I knew
a love I once lived for
now feelings untrue

I cried me a river
a stream of silent tears
I gave up my self-respect
I gave up the real me.

I Admit

Like you, I find it difficult to
say what's on my mind
much of the time
until, I can't keep it in
and there's the threat of exploding.
So, to you, I want to say
I am proud of you always.
I feel for you what I can't explain
and, it's a love so deep it burns with pain
because you're not ready
to make this steady
which would be so very good
and what many wish they could
find
in a lifetime--
if we'd just not be so scared
of this, which is so rare
and it's real...
I think you know the deal
that it's true, what you feel.
We want to stay in denial
that, maybe, it's a trial
draining it to the last drop
trying to make the truth stop
again
when will this end?

when we can be
with each other honestly
when there's no fear
and you won't avoid being near...
if it wasn't right
there'd be no fright
because, you can bet,
there'd be no threat.
But I just want you to know
I do love you so--
It's just hard to say
that I feel this way...
'cause, much like you
I admit...I'm afraid, too.

My Joy Stealer

You entered my life toting that smile
brightening where darkness once lay
Became a friend,
warmed the center of a spirit grown cold
Brought pleasure to an average day
Charming ways, a loving touch
All that was lacking
Natural attraction, deep affection
Something more we're becoming
My guard now down, closer than friends,
Your attention now slacking
You push me away
'cause we're too close
Standing in God's way
You took what you brought
Feelings slaughtered...
My joy stealer.

Happiness

There's just no true happiness, it seems
All it is is iridescent dreams
The warm arms that wrapped around me
Can only wrap me up generically
I left an area where I no longer fit
And you basically said I wasn't worth your kiss
But, your eyes said you're curious
Your hands wanted me near
Then, your mouth cuts me down
With words of no hope and insincere
But are we clear? Yeah.
There's no more happiness here
I wish I could disappear
But, I bet you wouldn't even notice
That I was no longer here.

Secrets and Lies

Words unspoken that hide the truth
Words that later don't come from you
Another innocently revealed the hidden
Talk from a distance relieve you the burden

Spoke words of praise for your honesty
To find there were secrets you were keeping from me
Feelings of trust laid aside
Anger, disappointment continue to rise

Why the secrets to cover your soul?
Wasn't our closeness enough to hold?...
Loved you so--lies shouldn't have been
Was here for you when pain lingered within

I'm hurting now, what else is untrue?
What kept you from telling what existed with you?
Anger, disappointment, hurt, disgust;
Wanting to scream from betrayal of trust

Was the love you exclaimed just the word of the day?
Next will you tell me you're giving it away?
Now know truth behind some deep looks from your eyes
Never once thought it was from secrets you hide
Do you know how it feels when news slaps in the face?

If it were you, could I keep my place?
For whatever we shared, its depth seemed deep
Said I'm amazing--wasn't I worth the keep?

All the love I deserve-- I thought I found within you
But, lies dull the heart--one I gave, one you took
Feel for you what no one else has had
That it's taken for granted makes the smile you love sad

Told you of the past, things I've been through
Told me you cared, but had to get yours in, too?
Loved you enough to be in love still
Let's be true to each other, sad spirits to kill

Daily prayers keep working--calmed this raging sea
Be the man you advertise, talk face to face with me
God saw fit your secrets afar revealed
Perhaps the distance was His best way to heal

I'd never condemn you for being human like me
But Honesty and Trust must exist, if we're to be
                        Because:
Secrets and lies will break a healed heart
Secrets and lies tear people apart.

Footprints

Excuse me...
Yeah, hi, it's me again.
You know, I saw you the other day....
You and your new girlfriend...
You know--the one you obviously thought
  could offer you more than me,
the one you had...
the one who loved you from the inside out.
Surely, she represents
a finer grade of woman than I, because
Surely, you wouldn't dare make yourself look bad
or humiliate me for something less.
Surely not...
Surely, you wouldn't risk losing me,
forever,
if it wasn't worth it.
Surely not...
Surely, you made your decision confidently.
You were sure.
But, yeah, I saw you the other morning.
I wanted to talk.
But, instead, I saw you and the one you chose
over me
walking--together.
I could only watch...
there was nothing I could do...

Make a scene?

No. Not me.

It was enough to be humiliated by you.

I didn't need to humiliate myself, too.

So, I just watched the two of you walk off together.

But, I was really with you, too, you know....

'Cause, as you were walking,

and I was watching,

I watched you walk away with

my heart

on

the bottom of your shoe...

leaving footprints of my tears.

I Wrote You

I wrote you my heart
when I put in into words
I needed to let you know
I'm trying to fight the urge
to tell you how I feel
With emotions you don't hear
I wish I could tell you
How much of a fool
I feel
I'm weary
waiting for you to notice me.

Where Will You Go?

The wind has slowed to a gentle breeze
Our tension has now been relieved
We couldn't make it work
There was too much hurt
around the love we thought we found
But, where will you go now?

Back to a familiar face
or a once known place?
Will you care for me still?
Even though we couldn't shelter how we both feel
I just want to know where you will go now,
And will it be sweeter to you somehow?

Best Friend

I found myself bearing my soul to you
Because I finally felt as if I could
You shared with me your secrets and dreams
Mutual desires to achieve as a team
The magic that stirred, no one could pretend
I waited forever for you—you were my best friend...

I'm so sorry it came to an end.

So You Thought...

You thought I said you were my man?
No, I don't think so.
See, my man would be good to me.
He wouldn't use me,
deny me
or take me for granted.
He would care for me,
love me,
appreciate me,
want me.
And, I would know it
'Cause, he would show it.

Where is the love, love?

Where is the love, love, when each of my teardrops spells
  out your name?
Loneliness is not supposed to exist when "I love you"
  is what you claim
Yet, when we've made it another 2 steps, there are 5 gone
  down the drain.
Where is the love then, love? Please tell me, why did it fade?

I cry out to you, yet my sorrow and fears are pushed away
I'm confused because the one who fills my heart keeps
  cutting it with the frozen edge of his pain
I am so empty, from my emotions running out of me like
  heavy, bleeding rains
Where is the love, now, love? Please tell me, why did it fade?

My days are endless nights with no bright lights on display
The depth of what I feel for you is numbed by the transfer of
  your pain
The sacrifice I made to care is a chance I took for life and
  always
So tell me, where is the love, then, love? And why in the world
  did it fade?

The colors your love and laughter showed me are suddenly
  turning grey
I find myself weeping, praying for you each night and day
Not having you to spend life with is a heartbreaking thought
  to face
So, please tell me, where did your love go, love, and why did
  you take it away?

Scars and Bruises

Cuts that no longer bleed
from the betrayal of needs
have become the scars
that are a semi-permanent part of me,
you see,
I've been misused, refused and emotionally abused
which caused pressure in my heart,
causing a big bruise
within me,
you see,
but the ointment, sedatives and eventually surgery
comes from a Doctor who's awesome and Heavenly
His ointment of healing closed many wounds
sedatives of peace calmed feelings of doom
and, surgery removed the broken parts, making more room
for the better things in life
which only come after I've survived
the strife
this one accuses
of causing many scars & bruises.

Blind Lover

Why does everyone else around me feel my sadness,
when the one I love is blind?
What do I need to do to get you to see it,
so we can put all the hurt behind?
I'm so tired of crying--what makes you treat me like you do?
I've tried to love you, let you know you're cared for,
and do what I can for you.
You deserve to have good things,
to be treated with the utmost respect.
At what point did my actions toward you say
I deserve so much less?
I remember the times you'd tell it to me,
that you never want to see me hurt.
Then why when I'm willing to work things out,
you turn around and treat me like dirt?
I've been struggling with life,
my days are sadder without any concern from you.
I want you to know how badly I feel,
I deserve none of this from you,
I'm the one who you've made a fool of and
that treatment to me, you are now due.
But I'm not that way, no matter what's happened,
I'll be the understanding one.

Because I believe in you, trust what's sincere,
and want to get past what's been done.
I'm so confused, I pray you'll care how I feel and won't kill
what already seems to be dying.
My world is crumbling, I thought you'd be different,
that our times wouldn't be this trying.
I need to be treated the way I deserve,
I've been so good to you.
I love you like you wouldn't believe, yet wonder if...
someday, I'll ever get the same, too.

Let It Go

You didn't really care for me,
and my heart was broken.
You had to share,
and make me your joke.

I gave you my all,
and it didn't even matter.
You didn't take seriously my fall,
which makes it all sadder.

What didn't satisfy you?
What made you stray?
What did the other do...
that made you turn away?

You never really tried to know me.
You didn't care why I hurt.
Yet, you claimed I made you happy--
but ended up treating me like dirt.

Now, much time has passed, and
God's put us back in touch...
I wonder how long this pain will last--
wishing it didn't still hurt so much.

You told me you missed me,
which was surprising to hear.
I almost thought I should believe you,
But, again, just felt the hurt from last year.

One more time, I'm disappointed.
I see how the past doesn't die.
I thought you were finally disjointed...
And, then, I saw you pass by.

The part of my memory I allowed to sleep
was jarred because you haven't let go yet.
The view of reality reached down deep--
And, again, my feelings were upset.

What's got you still holding on?
Relieve my curiosity.
I wish all my feelings for you were gone,
and that your not letting go wasn't another insult to me.

The Untruth Shall...

The bell rings
Game over
Time for your word to win with me
And what I mean is
That it's time that your word wins
With me
I mean that if you give me your word
It wins, 'cause it's the truth
The truth that comes from you
That means you've kept your word
That means you've lived what you've said
'Cause you're committed
Committed to the
Committed to the
Committed to your words
Which you have spoken to me
You see,
I have no more patience for untrue words
That come from you
Or those like you
'Cause see, that means if your words are untrue
You have no respect for me
You have no appreciation of me
Important, is not me

You have no real
Desire
For
Me
You don't take me seriously
What I mean is
You either take my interest for granted
Or
You don't really care if you keep me
'Cause your untrue words
Your uncommitted words
Your lack of respect for your own words
Will drive me away
And it's okay with you
Because they are not true
When they come from you
And the truth
The untruth
The untruth, my friend
Shall
Surely make me flee.

The Care Clock

It's too early for you to care, according to your clock...
Yes, I know,
You've already answered the question,
you've already checked the box
So, according to your schedule,
you'll know when to care for me
Because, surely God doesn't know what He's doing,
He doesn't supply our needs...
Yeah. Right.

I realize the day is early,
the sun hasn't begun to set
But, God's plans don't always fit our schedules
when He gives us what we get
Sometimes, when it's the wrong time to us,
His plan comes into true light
Sometimes, we plan for it tomorrow,
but He says, it's happening tonight.

So, when we deny a blessing
God sends sooner that we want Him to
It's like saying, "No thanks, God, I've got this one;
I can do this one without You."
So, my friend, when the alarm sounds and says,
yes, you may now care for me
I'm sorry, but you'll be too late
and I will only be your fantasy.

I Hate Loving You

I wish I hadn't felt your spirit
I wish I hadn't tasted your charm
I wish I hadn't wanted so badly to know
what it's like in your arms

You spoke words that moved me
like no other's ever have
But I won't be waiting for you
to want me just as bad

You say it's too soon to care for me
I wish you only knew
That tomorrow isn't promised
And how I hate loving you.

Rejected, Dejected, Affected

your livelihood keeps us at such a distance
and your fears and emotions create much resistance
I don't know how to really handle all of this
but, I do know your companionship, I miss
better communication is all it would take
to eliminate some of the distance we create
it shouldn't be too much to show each other we care
but, when it comes from one more than the other,
it isn't very fair
it makes one feel unwanted, undesired and
not thought much of
but, all I'm trying to do is share some of my
God-inspired love
If you'd allow it, you'd receive much
attention and affection
I think of you often and truly care,
but sadly, all I feel is rejection.

Sometimes...

sometimes I love you
sometimes I don't
sometimes you worry me
and my feelings are remote
sometimes I care if you live or you die
sometimes I have no idea why
sometimes you make me feel like I matter
sometimes I'm tempted to become a batterer
sometimes I appreciate being treated like a queen
sometimes I do wish you *were* just a dream
sometimes the future seems so distant
sometimes our union is not such a misfit
sometimes the darkness awakens from our light
and sometimes I don't want to rise from the night

sometimes I love you
and sometimes I don't

and sometimes you matter...
but someday you won't.

Empty

why must I continue to cry
and, feel like I die inside
I try to give up this pain
this emptiness
this feeling of being cast aside
but, it's still so much...
like a sore that never really heals...
But, you don't care how I feel.

Amnesia

I say I wish I never met you
They say to have loved at all is good
But they don't know this screaming heartache
And how I'd forget you, if I could.

Spring

❧❧

Rekindling

Spring is known to represent new birth, renewal, regeneration...well, re- or new *everything*. It's time to start over. We've defrosted from the cold reality of winter. We've survived the brutality of that change of season, and we've had time to refreshen our spirits, emotions and minds. Sometimes, the reality of where our hearts truly belong brings us to the realization that they never really left. Once the coldness of winter defrosts, what was seemingly lost or taken away sometimes returns--new, and ready to begin again. And, we return to what we knew...to give it another try.

2nd Chances

Fate has a way of providing
opportunity
when we mess up
the first time.
Sometimes, we're blind
we misuse
we neglect
we discard
that which was meant
for us the 1st time.
When it's gone
it's gone...
we've lost
we've failed
we forever regret.
Once in a while
what was sent by God
the 1st time
comes back around
to close the circle...
don't fight it
don't deny it
don't let it slip away.
Do what you must
because 2nd chances
don't come every day.

Show and Tell

Show me, if it's real--
These feelings you say you feel.
Love isn't only a word--
It should be shown and not just heard.

Tell me the things you keep in your heart--
The reasons you are willing to restart.
Please understand love is not just the words we speak.
It's action, performance and what you show me.

So, show and don't just tell me what I'm worth to you.
Let me see that being with me is something
you will now value.
I know we must take our time, but if you're sincere,
You'll gladly show and tell me your heart
just beats for me.

Not For Free

I'm so sorry
Baby
But, this body ain't free
This one you see
And want for company
But, it ain't free
And whether or not you agree
This is how it has to be...

So don't bother detaining
Cause I'm not explaining
Please save the tears like it's raining
And don't give me the story of how you're paining

'Cause like I said, this body ain't free
So there's no availability for your company
Unless you're prepared for the responsibility
Of what it takes to be with me

So, let me just cut to the chase
And save the time we'd waste
Now make sure you hear me
And listen as I start...
My company won't cost you money
Honey, it'll cost you your heart.

Post-Birthday Blues

I need to know from you
What you want with me--
What is it you want to do--
What do you want us to be.

We've been brought back into one another's lives
A sign that God is for real and true
I've forgiven you one more time
But, I'm not sure what we're trying to do.

Second chances don't always happen
Definitely not like this
You took me by surprise when
You said it's me you miss.

OK...so you miss me...
and you miss my company.
I missed you, too, especially when you were sweet
but not when you treated me disrespectfully.

I'm a grown woman--
and a lady, too.
I deserve the respect of a man
Most of all, I deserve much respect from you.

You are very special to me,
And, I thought of you often, too.
I deserve and demand to be pleased...
So, once and for all, treat me the way you want
    me to treat you.

Don't play head games with me.
I've earned much better than that.
If you do care and love me, be sincere--
or go somewhere else with your crap!

Free Me

Wishy washy ways
Never really worked for me
Instability and selfishness
No longer a commodity

If you can see through me
You're quite Godly
If you can still want me
Then you're worthy

Most don't want to be
In a place where the real me speaks
So, if you can appreciate that honestly
Then you deserve me

Wishy ways never worked for me
But that's what I've always received
The expected
The accepted
But, they never really worked for me

So, if you believe
You can offer me
Reality
Stability
Tranquility

In humility
While needing, craving
Wanting me
Then that's what will
Finally
Make me
Truly
Feel I'm free.

So...
What's it gonna be?

You Stir Me!

You stir me
Not like with a spoon
But with your words, your thoughts and your actions,

You stir me
So that the fruit at the bottom of my cup
blends together with my essence
making one smooth, flavorful combination.

Honey, you stir me
With your energy,
inspiring me to reach deep within my soul
where words and thoughts are nestled,
awaiting their turn to travel in another's heart.

You stir me
With your sweet sounding voice
that speaks what the blind man could not see

You stir me
with your heavenly, masculine self
which makes me truly enjoy being the woman I am.

Yes, you stir me!
Honey, you stir me!
Man, you just stir me up!

Golden Kisses

a kiss like gold is what I get from you
beyond its weight in richness
sparkles upon my lips
leaving me feeling priceless

a kiss like gold is what I get from you
pure and tempting in nature
welcomed and wanted
leaving me tranquilized and needing to be captured

your kiss is like gold to me
worth more than its weight in richness
and when you are absent from me
it's exactly what I'm missing.

Tomorrow

if tomorrow ended today
could you say you know what it's like to love me?
or that you've floated in my stream of kisses
or even tasted the fruit of my passion?
could you say you've slumbered in my wildest dreams
or that you've lounged lazily in my arms?
if tomorrow ended today
could you say you've enjoyed the ultimate feast
which is to be fed respect, appreciation, adoration
and elevation from my fingertips?

if tomorrow ended today
could you say you've enjoyed the hidden pleasures of life?
or that you've learned what it's like
to make another's dream come true?
could you say you've experienced a love so strong and
deep it shouted out loud yet needed no words?
if tomorrow ended today
could you say you've really, and I mean really,
experienced a toe-tingling, heart-pounding,
lip-smacking, eye-watering kind of love?

so, if tomorrow ended today
could you say...
could you say
you know what it's like
to love with me?

Again

If I could feel that joy from your smile
the warmth from your eyes
with the touch that soothed my spirit
and the kiss that filled my heart...

I would fall in love with you all over again.

Summer

❧

Passion

If you could drink from *my* fountain...

Yeah, *my* fountain. Enough said. What else *can* be said? Yes, it's all about passion, but also admiration, respect *and* appreciation, from all angles. This is when the fountain is full and flowing, and only one person is confident and trusting enough to accept that it is truly, completely and will be forever quenching. It's about recognizing and accepting the feelings that have evolved toward that one particular person. And, it's about enjoying that time and experience to the fullest. It's all about the passion that's within us all and having someONE special to share it all with. Yeah...It's the foundation of a love that's meant to last forever...and beyond.

EveryDay Love

Like the early morning mist and dew
Your EveryDay love refreshes and soothes
Then I feel the warmth of the sun
Wrapping me in the arms of your love
To brighten my every day
With a smile that says "I'll love you...always."

Loving You

when i'm holding you in my arms
i'm telling you how much i want you
when i'm looking into your eyes
i'm telling you i'm so proud of you
when i'm kissing you gently on the cheek
i'm telling you you are worthy
when i'm holding your hand in mine
it's because i feel your heart
when i sigh with deepness into your ear
it's because i'm loving you.

Soul Mate 1

I want to be your partner
Your friend
Your lover
The extension of your soul...

Your strength when you're feeling weak
When you're tired, my rest you'll seek
I want to be your confidence when you doubt
Your laughter when you're sad about
Your rescuer when you're burdened
Your smile when you're happy, not hurting
Your peace when you're anxious
And your wisdom when you're confused or impatient
I want to hold your hand when you're overwhelmed
Be your exhale when you're exhausted and worn
Your blanket when the world is cold
Your cool breeze when life gets too hot to hold
I want to be your shelter during life's worse storms
And your reservoir when it has drained you long

I want to be what no other person could ever be...
That's the love of God that flows through me freely...
And that's all I want you to have of me.

When I Think...

Sometimes, when i think hard enuf,
I can almost feel you next to me...
the warmth of your body.

Sometimes, when i think hard enuf,
I can almost feel the smoothness of your skin...
your gentle face beneath my fingertips.

Sometimes, when i think hard enuf,
I can almost see you in the dark...
the way you look into my eyes with much affection.

And, sometimes, when i think hard enuf,
I can almost feel your hands as they touch my skin...
you stroke my hair with passion.

And, sometimes, when i think hard enuf,
I can almost smell the sweet scent of your darkness...
the way your lips feel as you speak softly to me.

And, even sometimes, when i really think hard enuf,
I can almost feel the power of your embrace,
the release of energies as time slows down, and we
enter a place where all is silent and so very beautiful.

Your Love

I saw your love
when you gazed at me
when you laughed with me
when you talked with me

I felt your love
when you rejoiced with me
when you shared with me
when you hurt with me

I knew your love
when you gave your all to me.

Rendezvous

Rendezvous with you
Who
I see
In my dreams
To the extreme
Feeling your touch
Tasting your kiss
Making up for the time we've missed
Envisioning your face
With my eyes closed
Stealing your heart
Before you could know
Whispering your name
As you do the same
Because you feel just as I do
Yeah…'cause I sure love you, too.

lovely melodies

lovely melodies between you and me...
strumming and streaming every which way
laughter and loving ways of play
mystical magic makes love say
and sing some day songs that caress my face
harmony in your hands every shade but grey
lovely--just lovely your loving ways ...

call me

call me your date
call me your fate
call me your tease
call me with pleads
call me crazy
call me your "staying"
call me serenity
call me plenty, please
call me a purrer
call me your stirrer
call me for mixing
call me bewitching
call me boldly
call me sweetly
whispery or screamy
just make sure you call me.

Today, I Wanted You

I wanted you
to look into my eyes
while I look adoringly into yours
I wanted you
to caress my hands while we talk about our lives
I wanted you
to give me a long, lingering hug
with those soft kisses to my cheek I like so much
I wanted you
to lay here with me while I read my Black erotica out loud
I wanted you
to hold me in your arms
because it's the promise you failed to keep
when you made it
I wanted you
to remind me of why I love you anyway
I wanted you
to kiss my lips warmly
and act like you mean the lip talk you speak
I wanted you
to want to do all these things and more
just because you want me that way
But most of all, today,
I just wanted you.

Suggestive

I am enticing, inviting, enthralling, exciting
I will move you, school you, soothe you, cool you
I am your feast, your steam, your theme, your dream
I will feel you, heal you, steal you, reveal to you
That you taunt me, I caught you, you want me, I haunt you
So tease me, appease me, receive me, relieve me
Surreal, I feel, your will, you fill
Miss me, kiss me, lift me, fit me
Undress you, caress you, beset you, content you
Embrace me, you grace me, you alone are my ecstasy
Alluring, securing, assuring, enduring
A thrill, then chill, until we're fulfilled.

Fire and Desire

I feel your heat when you whisper my name
I'm smoldering, not wanting to be tamed
smoke rises when temperatures soar
friction causes me to want you more
the surface crackles with soft pops of relief
but tension increases beyond my belief
the desire so strong, I feel myself yearning
put out my flames before they start burning
heat so intense, warm skin now ignited
the stroke of your fingertips have me excited
wanting you so much to strike up the flames
fighting the passion, moaning your name
touching me gently, soft fingertips
feeling passion that's hard to resist
please put out these flames before I erupt
stifle me with the kisses I enjoy so much
I want to know my fire is your desire
show me how you'll raise my temperature
higher and higher...

Night Rain

Night rain
Heart pain
I loved you last night
And I'll never be the same.

Your Expressions

Your Expressions

About the Author

J. shepbyrd was born and raised in Brooklyn, New York and is the 2005 First Place winner of Ebony magazine's Gertrude Johnson Williams Writing Contest with her short story, "The Train Ride." She is a graduate of Tennessee State University (B.A. in English/Prof. Writing) and Peabody College at Vanderbilt University (M.Ed. in Reading Education). She is also the author of one self-published book of poetry, *A Peace of My Mind: Life and Love/Inspiration,* and is looking forward to the publication of novels, *Mirror, Mirror* and *A Dream is Just a Dream.*

A Note From the Author

Thank you so much for allowing me to share these thoughts with you. I hope you've enjoyed, been inspired and/or comforted by this collection of poetry. One thing I've learned from sharing my work is that my thoughts and feelings are never just my own. They often speak to and for others, which makes this poetry thing all worth the while. It means a lot, because I know how helpful it can be to know someone else can identify with what we've been or are going through. So, I do hope that by sharing some of my intrigue, heartbreak, and joy, you, too will begin a path toward emotional freedom and healing, if that's what you've been knowingly or unknowingly needing or seeking.

These words are definitely all straight from the heart, and as always, I encourage each of you to write out your own thoughts, whether or not you consider yourself a "poet" or "writer." Many of us mainly write for sanity-sake and not just because we want to put a poem in a book. Writing can help us to begin releasing the bondages of our wounded hearts and souls. Consider giving it a try, if you haven't already discovered the peace that comes from it.

Lastly, I'd love to hear from you, so please feel free to shoot me an email with your comments or questions. In the meantime, stay tuned....there will be more to come.

You may contact me at:
fs_info@bellsouth.net or visit http://www.fshepbyrd.com

www.ingramcontent.com/pod-product-compliance
Lightning Source LLC
Chambersburg PA
CBHW051847040426
42447CB00006B/732